MW00990310

Able Publishing
a division of Kent Creative, LLC.

Cover Art: the incomparable Jared Tuttle,
Jared Tuttle Illustration & Design

Illustrations: Pages 21, 68, 102, 158:
the magnificient Evelyne Park

All other illustrations: Dan Kent

You can follow Dan at:
twitter.com/thatdankent

@thatdankent

to Barbara

who exposes me
to so much beauty
that no earthly poet
could possibly keep up

Contents

coughing out the struggle dust

the diagnosis

when I was a little boy
doctors diagnosed me
with *Delayed Comprehension*

"What's *Delayed Comprehension*?"
man, it took me forever
to figure out what *that* meant

dogs and lawns

there is a quip
about dogs and lawns:

> you can have one,
> you can't have both.

for the upright man
of God, the choice
is plain. absolute.
indubitable.

lawns are a fool's
vanity, a dystopian
toil, a worthless crop.
it's what dogs have
been telling us all along.

the inner guide

we were waiting for someone,
don't remember who,
at this coffee shop
south of the river.
Marcus reaches up, touches
a COMMUNITY BOARD flyer —
Pepto-Bismol-pink paper
(with dangling numbers
all along the bottom)
advertising a FREE class,
offered by some blinkless
woman in Buddha pajamas:

FIND YOUR INNER GUIDE

"this might be just the thing
you've been looking for,"
Marcus says,
"maybe just what you need."

I shrug, pointing
to my open palm
(for emphasis)
and declare:

"never trust a guide
you're required to find."

the caveman

B says I'm a caveman and
she makes some good points:

1. I'm fascinated by fire
2. I get mad at gravity
3. I don't read warning labels
4. I use dirty dishes
5. I like to pee outside

so she wasn't surprised
when, as we surveyed
the back yard, I said:

"Lawns are dumb."

at first she rolled her eyes.
then she said,
"Well, I'd rather
have wild grass,
with wild flowers
than a manicured lawn."

"Me too!" I snorted.

then I stepped
to her side,
grunt-whispered:
"If Bar-bar-a
come to moun-tain,
Dan come out cave."

HATS

I wish I looked good in hats.
the classic hats (I think they're called
'Sinatras,' or 'Fredortas'), like those on
dapper gangsters, midnight walkers.

I wish I looked good in hats.
I'd wear one all the time—
to keep my eyes dry when I walk in the rain,
to keep good ideas from floating away,
to keep cold out, to keep heat in,
to give the impression I'm absolved of my sins,
to walk with resolve, like I've paid all my dues,
and that all my laments are the *good* kind of blues.

I wish I looked good in hats.
I'd wear one everywhere;
like soft armor to guard my heart
from the panic-lifestyle of the hassled masses,
from the back-patters of all the middle classes,
from vote-casters and their propaganda breaths,
from happiness-addicts and their invisible deaths.

I wish I looked good in hats, but when
I put one on it's like a throw-pillow
resting high atop a weeping willow;
my head looks overgrown
(it scares the cats!),
like all *my* thoughts are cold
and all *my* sins, un-atoned.
I wish I looked good in hats,

but I don't.

the feminist bias

She worked in a power plant,
in a control room, with walls
like some B-movie space ship—
buttons and switches, and
monitors and blinking lights
from the floor to the ceiling.

She'd work long long hours
(would come home at sunrise
when I was going off to school).
It was hard work, but far better
than working in the coal yard
(with the coal cars, and dozens
of tough-guy macho burn-outs
and all their idiot-whistles and
sexually suggestive gestures,
and horny-guy propositions).

Endless train cars full of coal,
when she worked in the yard,
would roll in along the tracks,
stopping over cavernous chutes
and she, with her great strength,
would hoist high the iron bar
(which weighed as much as she did),
and she'd swing the bar down
striking the lever, and coal would
explode out the bottom, down
the chute, and she'd stand there

in the black cloud, her muscles
glistening, until the next coal car
rolled into its position.

When she earned her promotion
to the space ship, most of those
macho tough-guys resented her.
She could do whatever they could
(that much was obvious, now),
and when she passed the tests,
it became clear: she could do more.
And all those men, most of whom
never offered her a lick of help,
now stood sheepish, empty headed,
as she hustled right-on past them,
leaving them all standing there
scratching beer bellies in her dust.

banana peels

she begs me not to leave
banana peels
on the countertop
(when I make my oatmeal).

"I don't," I say.
she gives me a look.
"well, maybe once I did."
she says I do it all the time.
I think she's losing her mind.

I get to work this morning,
she texts me:
good morning, sunshine.
I text back:
mornin' angel-flower.

then she texts me a picture
of a desecrated
banana peel
on the counter
(near my oatmeal bowl).

I've yet to reply.

mountains get bigger
the closer you get to them
monsters get smaller

the wrong pond

all I was doing was getting a book
(Kane's "The Significance of Free Will")
when a breathy voice rattled me
right outside the library doors.

"professor Kent, I was in your lecture,"
she said, "it really touched me."

I looked up, reorienting from deep,
abstract thought, to see a child-lady
half my age with two equally concrete
female friends.

"on the fear of the Lord,"
she said, realizing I had no clue.

"oh," I said, all three of them encroaching,
prompting me to calculate my age
"I'm so glad you got something out of it."

see, it's just *this* sort of moment that terrifies,
tantalizes, my male friends ('the guys').
when I say "I teach at the college," they say:
"How can you handle all those young women?"
"It's no big deal," I say, because it's not.

"well, it would drive me crazy,' they confess.

the gist of their concern, of course, is sexual
temptation and I tell them: "do the math.
there's no sense even *thinking* about sex—
none of that will ever happen—and even if
it did, it would all last, what, 5 minutes?
Your marriage covenant would turn to plastic,
your God covenant would turn Genesis 3:23."

"right, uh-huh," they scoff, and roll their eyes.

"listen, you have to flip a switch in your head.
they're fish in a pond that's no longer your pond.
they've their own pool of fish—their own men—
they don't belong to you, don't belong to me.
ya' gotta let them be."

"Uh-huh," the guys say.

"I hope you teach again, Mr Kent," she says.

"Thank you," I say, in a wholly flirtless way
(as if she was just some stranger in the park
who'd informed me that I'd dropped my keys)
and the three of them, with all their warm raw light,
walk away, and I'm glad they're gone (relieved!)
as I get tired, at this age, of sucking in my gut.

What a Pecker!

Ah, the Pileated Pecker—
a most striking bird.
So surgical,
what, with his precise extraction beak
and his diagnostic prowess
(he knows just where to make incisions).
He's theatrical, too,
what, with his Shakespearean crest
and his camera-ready poses.
And, he's industrial,
what, with his thunderous jackhammer head
and his midwestern work ethic.
You can hear him working all day,
like random machine gun bursts
echoing dreadful from concrete
remnants of some bombed out city.
What a bird! And he knows it, too!
He can't even wait to show himself off—
WukWukWukWukWukWukWukWuk
At 5:08 in the morning, while we lay
still embrangled in our lingering dreams.
WukWukWuk
Not far from our bedroom windows—
before we've even had our coffee or tea,
WukWukWukWuk
The Pileated Pecker.
we're all *so* impressed.

So very, very impressed.

I clean bathrooms

"Will you clean the bathroom," she asks
(she has visitors coming soon).
"Yeah, I'll clean the bathroom."
It grosses her out.
Doesn't bother me a bit.

In high school I worked at a bar,
a night club, full of hot shots.
It was called 'Hot Shots."
I was a bar-back, gopher, vomit cleaner.
Whenever some Tipsy-Todd erupted,
leaving a foul fun-puddle on the dance floor,
or by the pay phones, they'd call on me.
Clean that vomit will ya, they'd ask,
pointing to a spot.
It grossed them out.
Didn't bother me a bit.
The trick is to bury the repulsive lava
under something dry and neutral.
Kitty-litter works best.
I recommend 3 cups kitty-litter
for every 1 cup of sot-spew.

Anyway, I think how it worked was
some horny guy in his mating prime,
hypnotized by pompous aspirations,
would splash himself with about
a gallon-and-a-half of cologne—
Drakkar, Hugo Boss, or Sweet Fever—

He'd slick his hair back like he'd just fallen
from the sky and his hair was still blown back
except for 1 rope of hair, which dangled there
over his right eye, like cool chaos,
while his eggplant shirt, unbuttoned just so,
revealed his lowercase "t"
(can't bring myself to call it a Cross).
He shows his license,
pays the cover charge,
gets his hand stamped,
then blows into the club,
wide-eyed and optimistic.

But easy love is hard to catch,
and wires get crossed in his head,
and he convinces himself,
if there's any hope for action,
he's going to have to be far more interesting
than he currently is. So he slams
some hard liquor, making a big show of it,
and fills the air with "*Wooo-Hoos*" and raised fists,
then another shot, some ridiculous dancing
which includes showing off his 'shredded abs,'
another couple shots and, *dang,*
there's far more guys here than girls,
then more dancing, some dirty gestures,
another shot, and—*Uh-oh!*
He makes for the bathroom, but fails, and
all the fast drinking and erotic gyrations,

all the lame, hot-shot superficiality,
all the insecurity,
condense down
to an acrid bile,
which is rejected by his body
and his spirit,
and it lurches out
from deep inside of him
and all over the floor.

Then he looks at me, contrite, as if
he'd just now seen for the first time
how ridiculous he objectively is.
Sorry man, he says, knowing it's me
who'll be called upon to clean
the oozing carcass of his humiliation.

After college I worked on a geriatric unit
(mostly with Alzheimers patients)
Good job except I had to wipe butts.
The first time is the scariest, trying to
figure out how to press your hands
strategically between an old man's butt cheeks.
It's mushy. It stinks. It's intrusive.
It's gotta be done, though, so
you snap the rubber gloves,
grab the moist towelettes,
help the man up from the toilet,
position him before you properly—
bent forward, legs spread slightly—
and bring the towelette in low,

press in and wipe upwards,
starting near the testicles.
At that age, the cheeks are flabby
(the shit don't come off easy).
It's like trying to wipe
butterscotch pudding
off the top of a pan of Jello.

The men hate it so much and I understand.
These are men of action, some fought
in World War II, dodged land mines,
killed Nazis with their bare hands.
Some were farmers who conquered
Minnesota's cruel soil, and squeezed
food from dirt with their bare hands.
And now some blue-eyed bozo,
with a hair style and clean finger nails,
must take charge of their basic tasks?

Honestly, I came to appreciate it.
In a world of malingering sob stories
and bullshit panhandlers at every level,
wiping an old man's butt can be
somehow an honor—or, at least,
a refreshingly pure act of service.

"Will you clean the bathroom," she asks,
preparing the house for her book club.
It grosses her out.
"Yeah, I'll clean the bathroom."
Doesn't bother me a bit.

that ancient trick

I pull my chair to my screen
to face strange pages
of a half-written book
I have not seen
in many weeks
the words
I faintly recall but
where was I going?

What was the point?
or more pressing:
What was the *spirit*?
From where did I conjure this voice?

I know what needs to be done
that old magic
that dark ancient trick
(that I know not even how
but just know it happens
about seven layers down
my stratified mind)
where I close my eyes
flip some inner switches
and reopen
as some other persona

and just hope to God
it's the one who was writing
this mishmash before me.

**Robot with bow-tie
slowly approaching banana**

Looking Through Old Photos

Wow, this one is old.
I think that's a car,
or maybe a boat?
This pic's of me and my gramps.
Gosh, I remember that place.
Here's one of you at that camp.
Here's one before I gained weight.
Ah, dad always made that face.
Look! Here's the dog as a pup.
These old photos are great!
I love how they fade,
how they let go of their spot
in commune and time
at about the same rate
that they fade from our mind.

But nowadays,
in this digital age,
photos don't fade.

It's a blessing, I'm sure,
but also a shame.

We have to move on.
The puppy is gone.
Grandpa's not here.

I'm not the same.
The past is the past—
and should look that way.

But digital pics
are embalming the past—
electrified formaldehyde
refreshes the dead,
turns the fruit bowl to wax,
turns the flower to glass.

       Photos don't fade
       in the digital age.

We lose all sense
of passing time—
the gentle mercy
of distance.

We lose our own narrative flow.
History, frozen in that pose—
inverted rigor mortis:

       what's gone lives on and on,
       and we're the ones who can't let go.

no longer acquainted with the old ways

she dreads the dentist
so I drive her in
(Husband-of-the-Year, right?)
but like an idiot
I forget my phone

now I'm forced
to peruse dull
waiting-room
magazines

but I get all wrapped up
in this gripping story
with great illustrations
(I'm really into it!)
and I want to see more
so I extend a finger
down to the page
to touch the spot
but nothing happens —

"Did you just try to click
a magazine," she asks
restraining grand laughter

I sit straight
befuddled
try to construct
a plausible denial
but it's too late
for that kind of thing

she's laughing her brains out
and splashing my error
up and down
her Facebook stream

yeah yeah
go right ahead
laugh it up
ha ha ha
but I'm telling you:

it looked clickable.

My Wife is Making Me Old
(a birthday poem)

I woke up today,
43 for the first time.
My sweetie for my
birthday gave a kiss
throughout the day
for each short year
I've been here.
She kissed me all
over town. At least 5
kisses at the office
supply store (more
romantic than
you might think),
7 more at the used
book store
(she bought me
a collection of poems
by Wendell Berry),
like 9 more kisses
at the cafe
and dozens more
all along the way.

"I'm giving you a kiss
for ev'ry short year
you've been here
spinning
on this planet."

But she failed to plan it.
She tried to use
her fingers and toes,
but lost count along the line.

So when I awoke
I was 43.
When I layed down
that birthday night

I was 109.

the gift

mom got a thank-you card
from Dawn
thanking her for
a Christmas gift

"thank you all,"
the note said,
"for the Love Ball"

my mom was confused
and gave me a call
asked me if B or I
gave the Love Ball
to Dawn

"I don't even know—
what is that," I asked
as I typed it in
to Google

but all that came up
were sex toys
and discount DVDs
of I LOVE LUCY
starring
Lucille
Ball

"well, whatever it is,"
mom said,
"she really seems to like it."

the sneeze

back when I was a real
estate agent, not long ago,
in a big office, I'd work late
(usually typing away on some
writing project having nothing
to do with real estate).

there was this one time,
not sure why I'm thinking of it just now,
the building was empty but me
and a cleaning lady—all alone
in the maze of cubicles.

honestly, she was just my type
of workplace companion:
diligent, and not too beautiful.

anyway, at some point,
needing a synonym,
I opened my dusty thesaurus,
sneezed like a madman,
like a car bomb,
tossing my thoughts in the air,
jerking me in my chair,
and as I re-oriented I saw
the cleaning lady—obedient
to the spirit of some invisible religion—
traverse a sea of workspaces,
navigating desktops,
knocking over trash cans,

circumventing coat racks—
man-handled towards me
by some ancient superstition,
until she stood before me and said:

"BLESS YOU!"

"Thanks," I said,
then watched her
make her way across
the office wreckage,
the white-collar
obstacle course,
all the way back
to her vacuum and broom,
just as I felt the second sneeze coming on.

sneeze imitator

prospective buyers

what was really annoying
I'd run all over town
with prospective buyers
showing a thousand homes
and It was always the same
damn silly refrain:

> *open concept*
> *open concept*
> *we want open concept*
> *oooh, I like how open this is*
> *I love a open concept*
> *this is nice but I wonder*
> *can we make it open concept?*

Gawd, it was non-stop!
and all these builders
building new homes
everywhere I look
—why?
all you need to do:
put a toilet, sink, tub
in a prairie field
or a parking lot
brand it:

'OPEN CONCEPT'

you'll make millions!

Packing Heat

guns look so cool
(let's be honest).
I know, it's childish,
and not becoming
of a pacifist like me.

if only guns didn't kill.
if only guns shot peace!
—I'd pack that heat!

I'd come rushing in,
guns a' blazing,
shepherding corrective
explosions:

Blam! Blam!

puncturing holes
in pompous oppressors—
their smugness squeals
as it gushes, oozes
out their peace-holes,
converts to steam,
slithers along the floor boards,
disappears between the seams;

then after a minute or so
of redemptive agony,
the oppressor would leap

back to his feet,
with bounding cheer—
unseen (and unfelt)
in many'a year.

—Watch out!
in steps some
crazy-eyed Charlie Hustle,
looking to con
an unsuspecting,
vulnerable grandmother—

Blam! Blam!

he clutches his chest,
falls to the floor,
crawls out the door,
down the hot street,
into the arms of the wife
and child he left behind.

Blam! Blam!

righteous bullets
rupture steel wallets
of bloodless bankers, and
dollar bills explode into the sky,
metamorphosize
into butterflies,

flutter back to the soft pockets
of the swindled masses.

Blam! Blam!

hot lead through the heart
of each perfidious preacher,
lead so hot
it melts the White-Out
from the face of every
buried bible verse,
unleashing ancient light,
which explodes like a beacon
into the chapel's sky,
and hoards of God-seekers
pour into the pews
to find refreshment for
their thirsty souls.

Blam! Blam!

all over my wicked world,
shattering the fragile
masks of frightful
aggressors.

Blam! Blam!

anti-chaos!
calming!
settling!

comforting!
resolving!

Blam! Blam! Blam!

then I'd just stand
atop the debris,
firmly fixed
in the correctage
(inverse of *wreckage*)
looking oh-so cool
in the center
of the freshly quieted
scene, with a Clint
Eastwood squint,
and a prodigious
Peace Pistol in each
unwavering hand—
long, pointed pipes
of peaceful proactivity,
each one exhaling
the swirling smoke
of an action taken,
of threats inverted,
of goodness asserted.

The Angst and the Lament of the Internet Troll, Who Would Probably Complain to the Stewardess About the Coffee Even as the Airplane was Falling to Its Doom, and Who is but a Lie Shrouded in Decaying Matter, and Who Also Fritters His Talents Away Lulling Noble Revivals to Sleep, and Who Stumbles Around so Blindly He Can't Even Realize We Are ALL (Each of Us) Simply Beginners, Glad to Be Alive:

anger as big as the internet,
fists the size of microchips.

men shouldn't own guns
look at public toilet seats
there's piss ev'rywhere

The Narrator

Grandpa was a real gas
he had only one arm
fought in Korea

I remember
he used to narrate
his farts

with an elbow on the table
cigarette
between fingers
held up-and-out
before his plump nose

he'd lean to one cheek
release a long squeaker
like a rusty trumpet
blown by a toddler

then he'd say out loud
right at the moment
the fart ended:

"Done with that."

or

— fart —

"Don't need that anymore."

or

—   — fart — —   —

"That didn't sound right."

or

— fart —

"Hello! I wasn't expecting you."

or he'd sometimes get
the whole family involved like:

— fart — — — --

"There's a kiss for ya' Danny!"

I come from a long long line
of clever people.

sucks to be a house fly

busy busy busy
no time for silly
poetry
things to do
places to be—
yet can never get
where you're going
because
some wicked
or dim-witted
principality
or power
has erected
a perplexing kingdom
of invisible barriers
hey I get it
the poor flies
with mad ambition
smack the glass
again-and-again
and it hurts.
they press and press
it makes them sad
I understand
(I mean, really,
have *you* ever seen
a happy mime?)
but they don't quit
they buzz and bop

and crawl and slam
then fly away
a speck of rage
racing the cage
that is your house
on redundant tracks
dizzy circles
figure 8's
same old patterns
again and again
and I understand
you do what you know—
what else do you do?
"there's no way out"
they cry
but always give it
one more try

The Road Less Trampled

Two roads diverged in a yellow wood.
Mr. Frost could only travel one.
He stood a while to weigh his choice.
Then took the road less traveled by,
"And that has made all the difference"
(it all worked out, it all went well).
Ages and ages hence passed, and I,
too, came upon a crucial fork,
many paths, but could travel one.

With a sigh I shrugged, flipped a coin;
there are no roads less traveled by.
Each one's over-trodden, madly trampled.
A gajillion feet diffused on each.
No matter the path we know ev'ry bend.
No matter the path, we never get lost.
No matter the path, we know how it ends.
Travel's now sad, and life is a bore.
There are no paths, Mr Frost,
that make much difference.
Not any more.

ghosts are NOT scary
a world with only matter
—now THAT is scary

ear plugs
(for Ansel)

Sometimes I gotta'
wake at 4 a.m.
or sometimes 'those'
neighbors giggle
their pants off, rowdy
from fireworks (which shake
our windows).

I retaliate with
ear plugs. Blue ones.
Man, do I sleep deep—
like a rock in a clam
at the bottom of
the sea. I reuse
each ear plug.

But my screwball dog
has this freak-fetish:
he *eats* ear plugs!
Relishes them! Gets
hysterical over them. I
hide them, he finds them.
It's insane.

I place them outta'
reach, he devises
tactics to get them.
I'm competitive.
Ear Plugs is now my
favorite game, my
treasured toil.

A few days ago,
he died. In my arms.
We miss him so much.

My wife and I saw,
today, a poop-stained
ear plug (won't digest),
peeking up at us
from the sloppy grass.
Our faces got bright
and we laughed.

We huddled around,
gazing down, like we're
peering into the holy
cradle in the divine
manger. We even
took a dozen
pictures.

He meant to leave it —
to perpetuate
our favorite game —
beaming bright blue,
as if to say: "I won."
As if to say:
"I miss you, too."

heavenly clouds

she's searching the web
for near-death experiences—
ones that involve animals
(our dog died).
she's hunting for reassurance.
like maybe someone died
and saw their dog Chewy
running through a golden field.
or maybe someone's cat Patches
rubbed against their spirit-leg.
sadly all she's found are swads
and swads and swads of cliché
religious websites,
pushing cognitive candy,
false hope covered in frosting.
"of course your dog's in heaven,"
they say. "God wouldn't have it
any other way."

but she's the scientific type
and there's much at stake.
she wants evidence—even a trace!
she tells me:

> *"If the site has heavenly clouds*
> *in the background I know right away*
> *it's bullshit."*

I wish there were more believers like her.
I really do.

The Dead of the Leaves

The dead of the leaves
have covered the trees.
The reds from the greens
turn brown in the streets.

The simple are filled with glee
before the colorful trees,
suggesting: *this would not be
had death not come on the scene.*
But I remember the spring,
when the trees were merely green.

With life in the leaves
enriching the trees,
I'd rather have greens
than death in the streets.

reading poetry

I read Robert Frost
when things are well,
my complexion's good,
I'm eating right, exercising,
and things are all fine
between my Lord and I.

I read Dylan Thomas
when creativity's flat,
my words are soaked in piss,
when every thought's cliché
and I need mental dynamite
to shake my flow, stretch my reach.

I read Wendell Berry
in romantic mornings with my wife,
because he's so darn wholesome—
I'm hoping he prompts discussion
which pulls us from ourselves, then
pushes together our smitten hearts.

I read Charles Bukowski,
pants down, flaccid, on toilet,
wholly frank in fat and stance,
in earth's last place to be alone,
doing the most natural task:
diligently excreting waste.

Let's Not Get Ahead of Ourselves

some days
I doubt
eternality

infinite
tomorrows

days-upon-days
everlasting

oh of course
GOD is wholly
everlasting
(I'm not dumb)

he's up there
stoned on
immortality

and I get
his desire for
companionship—
to pass the time—
but with us?
forever?
I have doubts

I just left
this wooden
coffee shop

where a guy
went on and on and on and on
about stocks
passive income
getting rich

another was
really pissed
at something
for what?
who knows?
anyway
wanted me
pissed off too
but I wasn't —
so his anger grew

some days
I doubt
eternality
endless starts
without stops

it's just that
most people
get real dull
at about
ten minutes—
forty-five
minutes tops

Obligatory Snowman Poem

Back when the snow came down in sheets,
To bury deep the frightened streets,
And shook the spine of every tree,
All over this suburban sea,
The air was cold, the wind did pound,
And winter's white was all around,

The snow which filled some kids with glee,
Was packed into the shape of me.
With rocks for eyes, a hat for style,
Of course, the snowman's jolly smile.
And mighty sticks that I might wave,
And grass for hair (I'd rather shave).

With no agenda to complete,
But giving folks a jolly greet,
I found myself consumed in thought,
Of all that is and all that's not.
Because I think, I know I'm here.
But why not 'till just this past year?

Oh Dear! Are all those rumors true?
That snow gives way to morning dew?
And what, then, shall become of me?
I suppose that I'll atrophy
And flow down through the dirty street
In slush where spring and winter meet.

Well damn the hands that made this place!
That made this joy to build disgrace.
And made... Oh my, that breeze feels nice.
It gently cools my melting ice—
Which just prolongs my certain doom,
Like life had teased me in my tomb.

And damn the sun's agnostic glow—
Could melt me quick, but chooses slow.
I strain to raise a sagging eye
To kindly ask a passer-by,
"Pray tell me what the temp is, please."
"Why yes, it's thirty-three degrees."

Brrrrr, it's cold out there
Colder than a snowman's butt
Whaddya' do, though?

like fireflies dodging raindrops

the worm ~ ~

they say the early
bird will get her worm
you live and learn
you reject the herd
you speak out of turn
and the early bird
may well get her worm
but it's the late worm
who avoids the bird

THE SECRET TO MY SUCCESS:

I woke this morning
on my own, groggy mind,
sticky eyes, checked
my phone for the time—
38 seconds
before the alarm
would sound. I swiped it
OFF, rose to my feet,
and started my day—
38 seconds
ahead of schedule.

The girl is a bird. The world is her runway.

a girl the size of a sack
of potatoes, flower dress,
runs, if you can call it that
(still getting used to her feet),
more a drunken waddle-stomp,
but forward with fearless resolve,
with a desire that presses her abilities
to their utmost extremes—maybe beyond—
to mom's awaiting arms, who lifts her to the sky.

the choice

I do experiments
on suicidal people
(is that wrong?)
they come to me
at the hospital
"I wish I were dead,"
they say

"I have depression," they confess
and, more than anything, they
want me to believe them when
they tell me: "It's not my fault"

I ask them:

> if given a choice,
> would you *really*
> rather be dead,
>
> or
>
> would you rather get a chance
> to go back through life,
> to start over, to shrink
> to a child again,
> make new choices?

given these options
they almost never
choose death.

if your teacher throws
sodium chloride at you
call cops—that's a salt!

I dangle the candy worm
against the aquarium,
bumping the glass with it,
wiggling it, as the little fishies
shoot swiftly to position, floating
even, spread out in three-
dimensional auditorium
seating, each fish pointing
like featherless darts, tiny
torpedoes with blinkless eyes,
staring out the magic window, aimed
at the heart of the false treasure,
watching its every counterfeit
gyration, each hungry mouth opening,
closing, and opening and closing,
but saying absolutely nothing
at all.

social media

Things that see stars.

Saturday Morning Synchronicity
"Sarong Song"

Me? No. I'm too cheap to pay for parking.
Not for my bucket of bolts. No chance.
I just wait for a spot on the street.
I sit there (a hungry parking-vulture), waiting.
Waiting outside the building for a rodent
to scurry to a car and drive off. Funny thing,
this morning I was waiting behind a taxi,
sipping my coffee, windows down, Saturday
air blowing cool kisses before sunrise.
I was listening to an opera, of all things —
normally not my style, but it was good.
I even cranked up the volume as a voice,
bigger than a Friday night in June,
began probing her deep circumstance.
I watched the taxi driver, Somali guy,
check his watch about a hundred times
(I've no idea what *he* was listening to).
Anyway, a swarm of cellos erupted,
drowning the mood of a dancing flute,
just as this Somali gal approached the cab.
She knew the driver, that was obvious.
She leaned to the window as the singer
began slowly unpacking her stratified woe
(in an apocalyptic language only God knows).
The Somali woman, in bright garb, spat rapid
accusations while the taxi driver sank
low in his seat (given no chance to speak).
That's when the opera singer really began to peel
back the layers of her pain, as the Somali gal

unleashed the thesis of her prosecution, complete
with wild hand motions to invisible jurors.
Then bass drums banged as she backed away.
The taxi cab continued idling, coughing exhaust
in synch with the muted tremble of the engine,
and the relentlessness of the string section.

I was grasping the wheel, leaning forward
as she flung out her arms to make
her closing argument—which spread
her shaash wide like a terrifying cape,
like a psychedelic bird of prey—just as
the singer drilled into the frantic core
of her mighty feeling, and her voice
exploded, loud and long, piercing through
all the stones of her internal barricades.
What happened?
I knew nothing.
I knew everything!
The taxi slowly limped away, back into the city,
and the Somali woman marched into the building,
while withering violins escorted her down
to her new, smaller self, and her fresh start.
The music finally closed, on a major chord;
so as toilsome as it was, it was worth it—
and now, at the end,
she was
glad.

the prodigy

I'd be down there kneeling
on the carpet, leaning
on the coffee table, drawing
tigers or birds or writing
crazy action stories,
when keys would jangle
and scratch the door,
and mom swings in
with buzzing smiles,
followed by some guy
"This—this's Danny."
"Well hi'ya Danny,"
the man would say,
with widened eyes
and a pendulum grin
swinging back-n-forth
(this side to me, that side to mom).
Men in shoes.
Men in boots.
"Glad to meet you, Danny."
Men in vests.
Men in coats.
"Wow, did *you* draw that, Danny?"
Men with muscles.
Men with bellies.
Each new man my biggest fan.
I'd show them all
my drawings.
I'd read them all
my stories.

Men with watches.
Men with tattoos.
"You're a real prodigy,"
they'd say—whatever *that* means.

        In the morning, they'd be gone.

I'd amble out,
knuckles to eyes,
yawning and blinking,
drawings still spread out,
under beer cans,
under ashtrays—
looking wholly humdrum
in the sober light,
like litter in the auditorium
the morning after the big night.
Childish scratches.
Sloppy nonsense.
Boring triumphs.

Now, all these years later,
I'm somehow a grown up,
writing more complicated things,
tangled up in adult projects,

but still...

trying to impress the next guy
mom might bring through the door.

my first novel

wrote my first novel
before I had pubic hair
(I was 12)
hand-written
loose-leaf yellow
paper mangled
corners 20 pages long

mailed it to New York
DEL REY PUBLISHING
(I think they published
The Sword of Shannara)
the main guy
in my story
the hero
was brave
and clever
a bear attacked him
didn't panic though
just threw a banana
into a nearby bush
which intrigued the bear
who contracted his terrible roar
ambled to the bush
as the hero dashed
safely away

that's about all
that I recall
I wrote it

up north
at grandpa's cabin
I'd walk these long
dirt roads
alone
surrounded by miles
of old forest
and I'd wonder
"what's out there?"
probably lots of stuff
probably nothing much
there really were bears out there
(never saw one myself)
I did get friendly
with some deer though

anyway DEL REY
they wrote me back:

> 'Thanks for your
> submission.
> blah-blah-blah.
> we encourage you
> in your writing
> effort,
> but regret
> we are not
> considering
> material
> of this type

at this time.'

the jerks didn't even
return my novel
(it was my only copy)

I just hope
someone read it

It was good

My First Delusion

My first delusion was about
you — yes you, reading this
poem — well you and everyone really.
It happened when I was 5,
wily and spry, cute as a button.
I've no clue where the belief came from
(where do kids get such thoughts?).

The delusion was that people
appeared one way when I saw them,
but changed when I looked away.
The moment my eyes turned,
they became hideous beasts;
snarling, snotty monsters,
agitated by awkward appetites.

I *knew* it was true, I just needed *proof*.
So, for a good while, maybe even weeks,
you might see me (in town with mom
at the hardware store,
or at the city park
with the neighborhood kids),
spontaneously jerk around,
a spazz-crazed pirouette,
eyes locked on my suspect —
(I had to turn fast before they changed back).
They'd twitch, stand straight —
"Geez, what's wrong with you,"
they'd say, eyes wide, jaws dropped.
But I couldn't tell them nothing

or they'd know I was on to them.

I never caught any as monsters—
they switch back far too fast
(almost caught a lady once, though—
she was sniffing meat at the butcher).
Eventually, I quit my pursuit.
I must've thought: *If they work so hard*
to transform before I can catch them,
they must be somehow subject to me.
Plus, I was getting older, wiser—
normal life, out in plain sight,
was scary enough the way it was.

So I set myself to fighting
monsters I could see.

my calendar

my calendar's a wonderland
—black scratch marks shot
all across stacked boxes,
hotshot hieroglyphics,
private life-symbols,
guiding my visage
to my next most
enchanting
encounter
. . .

the art of war

Dave and Terri were moving
just across their street.
'Down-sizing'
(B and I and some other guys
and gals were helping).

We were taking a break
in the midday sun—
testing out their new porch.

Get to work, a passing helper
mocked as he carried a lamp
and shoe rack.

We're union, Bryan replied.

We'd been talking about cigars and
Dave lit one up, then told me his trick:

"The trick is to have a bunch of cheap cigars.
Give those to the guys, you know,
when you go to a thing.
Keep the good ones to yourself."

I raise my hand, for no reason:
"you mean like cannon fodder."

"Exactly," Dave says, "*exactly*."

"Right now I like these,"

he shows me a sheathed cigar.

HOYO de MONTERREY

"I think I've had one," I say, and,
"I like BACCARATs, but
I only smoke, like, 4 or 5 a year."

Then B chirps in: "You just told
Bryan you only smoke TWO cigars per year."
(this accusation is confirmed by Bryan)

Dave laughs, saying: "By dinner
he'll be smoking 5 per week!"

Then B flanks me: "You should hear
his fish stories."

They all had a real good laugh.
I was really really happy for them.

the thief

(Luke 23:40-42)

all my life it seems
there are these guys
they pop into my scenes
like bad ideas
in full flesh
reactive stances
stiff cold eyes
"fuck work" they say
"don't even go" or
"let's get drunk" or
"just take it" and
"what're they gonna' do?"

they're black holes
swallowing light
and you can bet they were right there hovering
around Jesus
in the market
on a hill
at the dock
"you should turn
the water into Vodka"
they'd say or
they'd drag
a massive basket
with one
tiny
grimy
coin

wedged in the wicker
at the dark bottom
"Jesus! Hey Jesus!
multiply this!"

these guys
they're inverted Pharisees
they shrug law
and catch no truth
when shepherds teach
their only power
is profanity
their only thrill
irreverence
they're dead on the inside
and on the out
they stand
open hands
at the parade
to be the first
to catch the candy
and the first
to mock and laugh
at the parade crash

but whaddya do?
have they any hope?

they let the absurd

gum-up their eyes
block out the light
until
"they know not what they do"

and there they stood
in the front row
of history's most grandiose parade crash
—the crucifixion—
after receiving bread and wine and fish
(crumbs still stuck in their beard hairs)
flush with derision
"if you're God, jump down!"
and "save yourself, magic-man!"
and "*you're* the king of the Jews?!"
and "do a trick for us Jesus!"
All of them thoroughly drunk
on contemptuous fun
all laughing at him
all scoffing at him
all mocking him
all hating him
all of them

except for one.

Church Music #1

(formerly: 'the hypocrite')

She's like me: dislikes church music.
    "Those songs are the same over
    and over and over—they
    get stuck in my head."
I'm nodding at her, and say:
"And the lyrics are often lousy."

The trees are greening nice
and you can't even see marsh
through the Dogwood brush.
"Doesn't that sound great,"
she says, eyes and mind wide,
tuned to a cacophony
of chirps and squeaks and eeps—
Towhees, Warblers, Pipits,
Starlings, and Nut-hatches.
Redundant melodies,
each with no more than 4
sharp notes stuck on repeat,
over and over and over and over and over,
from sunrise to sunset,
in the park, in the street,
in the yard, on the deck.
"You're such a hypocrite,"
I say (but don't mean it—
the music nature performs for God
has always been superior
to the bunglesome noise *we* make).

Church Music #3

We weren't even talking
about it, that's what I love
about her sometimes.
We were talking, I think,
about a better way to prep
bananas for compost;
the peels need to be diced.
It's just that they don't
compost if they're too big, and—
then she stops and says:

> *You should call your poem*
> *from yesterday 'Church Music'*
> *instead of 'the Hypocrite.'*
> *It's just that, 'the Hypocrite,'*
> *comes off harsh and the birds*
> *are the **real** church music.*

She's right, totally, but
she doesn't know I have this whole
other poem on church music.
I tell her I agree, but inside
I'm thinking: what should I call
the other? Church Music 2?
Poetry's so complicated.
As I think about that, I write this.
And what, then, shall I call this?

tragic bozos

I run into these tragic bozos—
never mind how, I just do.
this one guy, full of frowns
and dismissive shrugs,
lights a tough-guy cigarette,
blows smoke all over his stage,
pins me in one of his sad-traps:

"How many times can a man kill himself?"
I play along, knowing full well
it's a dumb trap: "Just once."
He huffs, gazes past me,
squints his sorrow, sneers
his dread, milks his angst,
then inflates and gets all clever:

"I've killed myself a hundred times, at least."
Then he gives me this pose,
like I'm s'posed to unfold
my easel to paint a portrait of his woe.
But I don't. I just say: "Killing yourself
doesn't seem to be working.
You should try something new."

when my wife comes home

her lemon-drop car
putters up the drive
and into the garage
I dash to the couch
grab pants off floor
yank them up over
my red undershorts
gather up the bottles
put them in the paper bag
hurry to the bathroom
push the seat down
let out a glorious burp
which I transform into
a talkative robot
(she hates when I do this)
and just like that
I am presentable and
the home is 'ours' again
and I greet her as she enters
with smiles and hugs and kisses.

people are like poems

people are like poems.
they go down easier if:
    they're not too wordy
    they're true
    they're self-deprecating
    they have a point
    and, if possible, a punchline.

worship service at a small, upstart church

I'm looking to you, Lord,
eyes to the rafters, singing
with my shy voice
in this rented chapel
as kids shriek and writhe,
like drunken warblers,
animated by the torture
of God-level boredom,
agitated by the vacuum
of mom & dad's divided
attentions—oh, the angst
of the lack of eyes
to a child!

Me?

I've got one eye high,
the other low, on heroic
parents, who worship you
with jerking and bending
and twitching and straying
faces, as they lunge and grab
and try to corral
their drunken warblers—
swirling, pulsating orbs
of atomic energy, each
on the brink of some
cataclysmic event—
something biblical, even—
perhaps **E X P L O D I N G**

any moment,
blowing these oak pews
through those stained
glass portals, like shards
of prophecy, to disrupt
the democratic kingdoms
of self-assured city
planners (who'll weep
and gnash chemically
whitened teeth).

You are a Lord of peace,
and I try to keep up
as the worship song
quickens to a close,
and the children
are released (unleashed?)
from the chapel,
into Sunday school
(or some other chamber
where their threat
can be contained).

a lady at a church

my wife had a dream
with symbols & layers
and rushing scenes
in concentric circles
which she traversed
down to the inner core
the center of the center
where a windowless church
stood like a block of secrets
and in the core of the church
an old lady deep in prayer
who turned to my wife
(who'd come so very far)
and said in a voice
like a secret mother:

It's just a life.
It doesn't have to be
perfect.

on eating healthy

buddy of mine
and I
were talking.
we've both made
changes.

eating less meat
more veggies
rice oatmeal beans
stuff like that
eating things God
made us to eat.

as for him,
he wants to see
his girls
(he has 4 of them)
grow up
get married

as for me,
I've got 9 books
I want to write
before I die.

you get to a certain age
you need to have
reasons.

Church Music #2

I've a confession
(I need help):
church music bothers me
don't get me wrong
it's not about God—
he's more than worthy and
everything I do and make—
my poems
my stories
my doodles
my tweets
my bonfires
my sandwiches...
it's all meant to praise Him
(it's all just crayon drawings
I hope God puts on his fridge)
but church music bugs me
I find my place in the pew
give a wave to Gary
nod to Toby and Sharon
and sit there among neighbors
brothers and sisters
fellow human beings
until —ZAP!— the lights dim
the synth kicks in
everyone shoots to their feet
looking forward blinkless
their expressions fix
they start to sing
and now they're all strangers

aliens from some strange place
an animated zombie army
(it's creepy, truthfully)
singing singing singing
simplistic monotonous songs
voices rise and rise
pretending to transcend
synthesizers whine
thick with emotion
and the zombie army react as planned
full of painful expressions
contrived affects
dramatic gestures
it all pulls on me
compels me to posture
but I refuse to give in
I'm too stubborn
or too sinful
or too skeptical
or too German
or too aware of my morning breath
or aware of my wrinkled clothes
I don't even know
I stand there unmoved
overthinking lyrics
until I lose interest
and stare off into ambiance
through strategic darkness
through fog-machine fog
through fancy lighting effects

and see a bright red EXIT sign
and remember going to a bondage bar
for a co-worker's birthday
one of those kinky places
with leather and chains
and whips and lace
and sorry flops acting like sex slaves
and bendy folks in cages
dangling from the ceiling
and horny dopes needing spankings
and old dudes who need shame
just to get an erection
and pulpits and upside down
crosses and wicked lighting
and fog-machine fog and—
a bright red EXIT sign
like a window in a movie theater
letting bright beams of reality
shine into the false ambiance
piercing through the poppycock
lowering a ladder to me upon which I climb
and curl up deep inside the warm red glow
until the absurdity washes over
until the superficial show ends
until the sermon begins
and all the zombies
become people again.

how to avoid the fools of April

let me start out by saying:
I HATE APRIL FOOLS DAY.
What a dumb thing.
Don't we have enough bullshit,
in this life, to detect as it is?
So, this year, I found a place to hide
from the stupidity.
I worked. 16 hour shift.
on a locked mental ward
behind 2 levels of electromagnetic doors.
Oh, coworkers still snuck
the imbecility in, no doubt
—trying to trick everyone silly,
but, on this April Fool's Day,
I stuck close to the hassled folks,
each with good cause to think
their fantastic falsehoods are true.

> One heard Barack Obama
> whispering in the vents.
> One was melting.
> One was Jesus.
> One was the reincarnation
> of Mahatma Gandhi.
> One was a supposed lover
> of Tori Spelling.

I stuck close to *them*,
because sometimes psychosis
is a strange kind of truth.

Live Trap

in our house we love
all critters, no matter
the size. We love bugs
and frogs and squirrels
and rabbits—yes
I know, it can be
nauseating

we have a paper cup
with a postcard lid
for catching spiders
and Boxelder bugs
so we can escort them
out of the house
unharmed

even mice (for *gawd's* sake)
we use *live-traps*
—little black boxes
big as a Study Bible
with a door contraption
let's the mouse in
won't let her out
she follows a dark
maze to a bread-blob
with peanut butter

she sits there all night

thinking and eating
frighten'd and pooping
just imagining all
her potential dooms
then (hours later) the box
moves rises shifts tilts
humans cackle with
clumsy hands (that's us
as we lift our catch)

"Her name is Sunny,"
my wife says—yes we
name every mouse

we bring Sunny
out to an open field
near some trees
bend down and lift
the black box lid
pour her out into dew-
covered grass
unsteady
disoriented
the shock of sunlight
then terror
she bolts
toward some shrubs
stops to look back at us
smiles (we assume)
smells the air to understand
what strange thing

has happen'd to her here—

mercy

then she's gone
through the woods
into the unknown—
out there with the rest of us
out into that stranger
and much larger
live trap

diamonds on dimes

the concerned citizen
backs his car from out
the third garage stall
clicks a steering wheel button
an oak and iron door closes
as our concerned citizen
circumnavigates the turnabout
around the greco fountain
then out through the iron gates
into the community
he touches a screen
Wagner (pronounced 'Vog-nur')
charges his ambiance as
he reaches down for his coffee
sips and sees some wear
on the sleeve of his Brioni shirt
he touches a button on his wheel
Have Davey replace shirts, he says
into some unseen microphone
our concerned citizen
now enters the city
rolls up his windows
vagrants walk without cause
ineffective folks gaze at him
as he slowly rolls by
all the way to city hall
he parks where he chooses
steps out and straightens himself
flattens his attire
squeezes his key with a ***CHIRP-BEEP***

as his car flickers and locks
he enters the government building
he enters the big room
where a large crowd is gathered
they're awkward
they're angry
they're active
they're dressed like slobs
they're ineffective
they're entitled
they're shouting laments
and our concerned citizen
(not even sure what their banter is about)
inhales to supply his voice
then bellows out above the crowd:

BUT WHO'S GOING TO PAY FOR IT!

he then returns to his car
drives back to his house
the one on the hill
overlooking the sea
parks in the garage
goes to his bar
mixes a drink
sits out on the deck
takes in the scene—
the sunlight sparkles
off the top of the waves
so lovely this time of day—
like diamonds on dimes.

The Blame

A violent storm far out at sea,
Upon an island with a tree,
Left for life but only three,
Who now lamented in the heat.
One Steve,
One Lee,
One Pete.
All hope of rescue obsolete.

A sickening stench intensely reeked,
Upon the island with a tree,
Which drove to madness all the three.
So quick the blame was cast on Steve.
They heaved,
And beat
Poor Steve
'Till death, then sank him in the sea.

It seemed then clear the smell was Lee,
Upon the island with a tree,
Provoking Pete to kill from need,
To cleanse the island of the stink.
He heaved,
And beat
Poor Lee
'till death, then sank him in the sea.

Ridden with guilt became of Pete,
Upon the island with a tree,
Who tied a boulder to his knee,
Then brought himself into the deep.
And screamed
"The stink!
It's ME!"
Then sank himself into the sea.

A violent storm far out at sea,
Upon an island with a tree,
Left for life but only three,
Who cast each other to the deep.
Poor Steve.
Poor Lee.
Poor Pete.
For all that time it was the tree.

one day at the beach

The world lowers it's gun.
My work, for now, is done.
I thought this world was gray,
And drains one's life away?
But such decay and blight
Was now nowhere in sight.

For all I saw was sun
And people having fun.
And all I felt was peace,
And gave my fears release.
And thought that I was wrong
To think my life too long.

Then, there beyond the trees,
The clouds had been released.
Everyone was hiding.
People were dividing.
Rain made each a stranger.
Turning peace to danger.

It's pointless to complain—
Too taxing on the brain.
This world of solid gray
Deceived me all the day.
Should time allow me then,
I'll be deceived again.

A great reunion
Jesus and his disciples
I'll set the table

shaking loose the blindfolds

NEUROBIOLOGY

Oh troubled cell—
So small, so light—
That makes me yell
And makes me fight.

teeth

B cracked a tooth
a piece fell out
same thing happened
not long ago to me

we're falling apart
from the inside out
the road is rough
life is long
things shake loose
all that stuff

the hope is to love
the parts that remain
be never bereft
(what can we do?
things that we lose
we cannot prevent)
and hope that she'll love
in me what is left
as I what's left in her—
now, at ninety-nine
point nine percent

oatmeal on the deck

I ate my oatmeal
out on the deck
in robe and slipper
early this morning.

I watched a frisky
bunny fall in love
with a speedy girl
who ran away.

he chased after her.
"It's too early," she said
(hadn't showered yet
or put makeup on).

he chased after her
anyway, stumbled,
fell face-first,
awkwardly.

the studio audience
of birds couldn't stop
laughing while an airplane
roared overhead.

the suckers

I'm a sucker,
you know,
for Design
Arguments
(or Teleological
Arguments—if
technical language
turns you on).

All of earth's
systems 'n critters
burst with intention,
overflow with genius
solutions to
tricky problems.

                Design's everywhere!

Blow-fish and their
big inflations,
Butterflies double-
sanctifications;
Cicadas and their
resurrections.
Porcupines and their
sharp protections
Kangaroos with
cozy pockets;
Gannets dive like
blazing rockets.

Cheetahs and their
sudden starts.
Giraffes with their
second hearts.
Puppies and their
wagging tails.
Blasting geysers
on Humpback whales.

Bible-Thumpers got
one thing right:

> *you find design*
> *wherever you look.*

I only wish
one simple thing
(I shouldn't even
have to say it):

> that all those thumpers
> (who defend design
> in nature more
> than anyone else I know)
> would then also
> defend (with equal
> pomp & passion)
>
> nature *itself*.

Evolution and It's Implications

"If you want to make your smoothie,"
she says, "I bought a banana bunch."
It was Independence Day,
an hour or so before lunch.

"We'll need more than *that*," I say.
She huffs, shakes her head, says:
"You go through SO many bananas."

She's right.

I use one in my oatmeal every day,
a couple more in my smoothie—
and what can I say? It all adds up.
ONE banana bunch is simply not enough.
But she doesn't seem to understand.
Sunshine engulfs her in warm light
as she looks up at me perplexed,
shading her eyes, and I realize
it is I who must bring light.

I say: "You do know we evolved
from monkeys and apes, right?"
The weight of my argument hits hard.
She drops her hand and looks away.
"I should've bought two," she says, contrite.

the cush

I waited at a coffee shop
down I plopped
into a cushy chair
and simply stared
at the flow
the 'on-the-go'
the 'in-the-know'
one would exit, three would enter
one more in, two more out
a commerce carousel
checklist-chasers
somehow
fitting it all in
getting it all done
daily planners in their hands
or on their phones
barking demands
throwing stones
pestered by the pull
jostled by the push
passing back-and-forth
as I sank into the cush
deeper—to their knees
deeper—to their feet
and looked up at them
so very tall with so much zeal
yet I'm not small
in fact I feel
(at this time)
above them all.

I'm glad I had toys as a child

what was I saying?
I lost my train of thought
—oh I was at the coffee shop
a girl and her grandma
burst into the store

grandma was an eyeful
ample girth draped in colors
decisive in her every move
whose dad I can only assume
was a bulldozer and
whose mom was a chandelier

the girl was typical
girly dress and girly shoes
maybe six or eight years old
pushed and corralled
by grandma who
cut in line when a customer
looked the other way

"Give me a large caramel latte,"
she said as the girl tugged
and muttered something up
"No, no, not after your behavior,"
grandma said and, "you have juice
out in the car."

nasty woman, I thought
but couldn't take my eyes off

"This is a HOT latte," she barked
as the barista handed her a mug
"I clearly said 'iced' (she didn't)
and don't scrimp on the whip."

the girl tugged Grandma's dress.
"Gramma can we go back to the store?"

grandma almost inhaled the room
"Oh, gawd, not this again,
no
we
can
not."

the girl then professed her love for a toy

"Well, you can't get ev'rything you want
that's life and you have to learn."

a barista handed grandma
her revised beverage
and grandma nudged and prodded
the disappointed girl along
in front of me as grandma
made her closing point:

"I never had toys when I was young
and I turned out just fine."

Spider changing her contact lenses

windows

I look out too many windows
(it diminishes my thrive).
Why chase just one thing
When I could chase five?

I start too many projects
(I've got lists of all my lists).
I work until I can't—
Until the strength escapes my fists.

Why do I sabotage my efforts
with my unholy hocus-pocus?
I'd be a great deal happier
If I could force myself to focus.

Pawned

The clock just ticks too fast.
"I'm sorry that I'm late."
The best of days have passed,
And those days weren't that great.

"I work so hard I'm ill,"
And older than my age.
The total of my bill
Is twice that of my wage.

I think the scales are *fixed*—
"Something is unfair."
Even the baby kicks—
a prenatal despair?

This life can taint one's sight.
"I shouldn't even look."
But I'm too dazed to fight.
The pawn could take my rook.

the goo

depression is gelatinous goo
it fills the portal door
but you can make it through

    and when you finally do
    you'll find a better you
    than the you you were before

priests could've been good
they should've masturbated
left the kids alone

not everything you need to know
is written in the Bible

it's hot out.
not too hot, though.
if you're just walking
from here to there
paced and steady
as an animatronic puppet
at some kiddie carnival
then no big deal

but if you so much as scratch
your ass too fast
you'll ooze with sweat

life is much about
maintaining the right pace
according to the heat

whatever heat you're in

No !

I'm throwing 'no'
ev'rywhere I go,
like a machine gun:
—no-no-no-no-no !

Some Billy Brightside
emerges from the daffodils:
"Avoid negative people."
—NO!

Some Charlie Hustle,
with energy-drink eyes:
"Outwork ev'ryone."
—NO!

Some Sally Sluffoff
glides in on a surf board:
"Live every day like it's your last."
—NO!

Some Harry Hopeful,
teetering from the ladder:
"Take it to the next level."
—NO!

Some Danny Dreamer,
distracted by butterflies:

"Think outside the box."
—NO!

Life is a strange parade
with wannabe gurus
throwing nuggets from their sack—
little chunks of bad idea
like cheap candy—
as they slowly float by.
But I'm not eating any of it—
in fact, I'm throwing it back.

Halloween 2007

The Lords of Autumn scrape their feet
Through sticks and leaves,
With paint and fangs,
With swords and sheets.

A 4-foot pirate looks at me,
What are you supposed to be?

Me? With my projects and thoughts?
With my pointless paths?
And my mental clots?
And my endless tasks?

A childish specter looks at me:
What are you supposed to be?

Me? With my fruitless wander?
With my wayward desires?
"I'm just a grasshopper, kid,
escaping through a forest fire."

A little witch looks up at me:
What are you supposed to be?

Me? With my thoughts on God?
With my urge to fight?
"I'm just a depraved moth
In desperate flight,

Searching for the source of troth,
Investigating rumors of light."

The Lords of Autumn scrape their feet
Through sticks and leaves,
With paint and fangs,
With swords and sheets.

What are you supposed to be?
Asks a hooded elf.

"I think this year I'll be myself."

the pilot

I called myself *investor*.
(I was a gambler).
I thought I was a *traveler*.
(I was a rambler).
Now I'm feeding birds
on a park bench.
A clumsy boy is running,
flying his kite.
He thinks he's the pilot—
And, for now, he's right.

a duck in the tree

how'm I supposed to write
a poem today?
I've nothing to say.
it was there, though,
in a disposable moment,
I had it—the insight.
I had it—the answer.
it aged to form
at the culmination
of a gem of a dream.
then I lost it.
a clattering garbage truck,
collecting up waste,
jiggled it from my grasp,
waking me from the scene.
what was it? what was it?
damn, what a waste.
I step out into the somber spring—
wet, cold, and gray
as an old diaper thrown away.
but there's a duck in the tree
up higher than a duck should be
looking down at me.
"Don't *you* have a good spot,"
I say, and wonder why the duck
should be sitting up in a tree.
the coffee shop is packed.
shoulders and purses everywhere.
two guys hide behind newspapers
feeding their omniscience, and they

trade treasures with each other.

You hear about Hernandez?
Who?
Hot-shot football guy. Millionaire.
Yeah?
Killed a guy. Now he killed himself.
They found him in his jail cell.
He had it all. It was his. He lost it.
Yeah? That's nothing.
You hear about this garbage tsunami?
A what!
Mountain of garbage in Sri Lanka
collapsed, crushing houses,
killed thirty villagers.

So much waste!

on my way home I wanted to see
the duck in the tree,
but she was gone.
she was there, though, I swear,
for a distinct and lucid time,
just sitting there looking down at me.
I swallowed my coffee drink,
felt the kick, felt the power,
surveyed my notebook,
pointed my pen,
wrote nothing.
damn, what a waste.
How'm I supposed to write
a poem today?

ministry break

Sister Mary Holstrom
takes a ministry break
out by the freethinking
rejects.

Sister Holstrom sucks
a cigerrette—smooth
flavored moments of
reflection.

Servants lose their energy.
"Holy Spirit come to me."
Mary doesn't inhale or
exhale.

She lets the embered stick
dangle from her parted lips.
She stokes her habit in her
habit.

Passer-bys feel compelled
to watch the smoking nun.
She sees the sadness thru the
laughter.

"Father, teaching monsters
to love is exhausting,"
she prays as she takes
a drag.

"Comforting dragons tires me." She doesn't move her face for several minutes.

A chunk of ash flutters off her chest, falling like gentle snowflakes to the concrete.

The streetlights kick on. Ambulance sirens lament somewhere distant.

Sister Mary smooshes the cigarette under her shoe, looks up, mutters: "mercy me."

GUY WITH A TRUCK

all I had was an old truck
no job
no gal
no plans
no cash
the country was wrecked
by big-shot investors
or was it politicians?
(I can't recall just now
whose turn it was
to do the wrecking)
anyway people were gaga
over craigslist dot com
selling sofas
buying bookshelves
trading ladders for wheel barrows
most of these folks
were hipsters
or homemakers
who rode buses or bicycles
or drove cars no bigger than stoves

I saw a need
an opportunity

I created an ad:

GUY WITH A TRUCK.
YOU NEED SOMETHING
HAULED, MOVED,
RUN OVER
OR HONKED AT,
CALL DAN,
651-98
3-4142

It was a hit!
I made like eight grand
in two months
Adam Smith
would've been proud
I was thrilled
life was a brand new
streetlight and I
was the only moth
but soon
very soon
other moths appeared
business diminished
ev'ry Chuck with a truck

was offering to haul
your table and chairs
your pile of bricks
your railing for stairs
for half the cost!

I pulled the ad
the thrill was gone
the light was lost
I was slapped away
by invisible hands
as the great council
of dead economists
gazed down at me
through a hole in the sky
and laughed.

Car for the Blind

the jazz I like

stumbling feathery percussion
bass guitars like demonic morse code
piano hopping around happy—
but not *too* happy
(in reach of mania,
never quite there)

that's the jazz I like
mood with no trauma
clean rhythm
erratic melody
always on the verge of jubilance
always on the verge of melancholy

jazz that pours over the moment
but does not abduct it
demands no allegiance
does not get offended if we look away
jazz that floats there like a ready friend

jazz—and this is important—
with NO goddamn horns
(okay, sure, the slow rusty horns
that moan like sad, drunk
bumblebees—those horns are fine)
but horns are always a risk

they always blow the same
they come promising thrills
all peppy and giggly

and escalating until
that moment your guard drops
then it's all shrieks and shrills
and the party stops

it's always the same build
it's always the same scam
it's meant to mimic
sexual arousal
louder sharper **higher** **higher**   **HIGHER**
beads of sweat and swollen cheeks
inflate the horn
blower's face
until he reaches peak-screech
until that crippling climax
that awful ear-gasm
that bends you over
that makes you wince
that startles your heart

until mercifully
the horn can blow no more
and you try to return
to whoever you were
to wherever you were
back to the start
before the assault
(the horny violation)
blew it all apart

Comey Hearing

I'm still in my boxers
watching congress question
James Comey (fired FBI
director) on CNN dot com
ties and microphones everywhere
politicians speaking clearly
sipping water
a r t i c u l a t i n g
holding up documents

    I'm picking a zit on my nose
    and sipping a latte through a straw,
    totally captivated by it all.

shifting explanations
secret investigations
salacious and unverified materials
"I can't answer that because it's classified."
strategic leaks
important memos
special committees
"Given what I knew, I acted accordingly."
Russian interferences

    —my butt itches and I remember:
    I'm out of clean clothes and I'll
    have to wear *these* boxers again.

"I won't comment on that in public."
back-door communication channels
false statements

suspicious ambassadors
discrete events
"I can't agree to that level of detail."

I take a HUGE bite of an apple,
toss the core into my overflowing
trashcan, which erupts
with a cloud of fruit flies.

slippery slopes
strategic compliments
"I won't feed into that cloud of suspicion."

It's all fascinating as hell
how intricate and tangled
the politics are and how subtle and
how indirect the accusations are
and just how masterful and civilized
plausible deniability can be
(I'm truly dazzled) but
as my straw burbles along
the empty bottom of my latte
I close my browser—
I have my own masters to answer to
and I'm far too busy
to fritter away my day
on the complicated dramas
of the principalities and powers
of earth's most recent
crumbling kingdom.

batty tenants

Did I tell you?
I built a bat box.
A fancy little house
for bats.

Made it from reclaimed
Cedar planks.
Absolutely gorgeous
in that rustic sort of way.

We're hoping to host bats
(we like them and they eat mosquitos).
But I gotta tell ya,
they're already a pain in the ass.

Their house must be painted black
(we gotta paint over the Cedar).
And they like facing south or east
(*southeast* being their ideal pref'rence)

Oh, and it must be 10 feet
off the ground
and at the very least, 20 feet
from any tree.
Shade is unacceptable—
full sun exposure only.

And the house must be near
a body of water—
preferably swamp or marsh.

Geez!

I once owned 4 rental homes,
had a hundred renters,
you take ALL of those combined—
Less demanding than this!

But I hope we get some bats.
I hope they make a life
they like in their little home.
And every once in a while,
come out to say hello.

customer service

went to Office Max
my mouse was shot
(defective clicker)
they had a big sale
on whimsical statues
I bought two
(they made me smile)
one an exclamation mark
the other a hashtag

at the purchase-counter
my items were shot
with a scanner gun and
the money-taking lady
looked me in the eye:
did you find what you were looking for?

it was a tough question
life is long and I'd come so far
I looked at the mouse
I looked at the hashtag
I looked at the exclamation mark
shrugged my retort:
"What more could I ask for?"

switching majors

at the start it was
Creative Writing

after just one class
I switched

I saw it clear:
these plucky young keyboard thumpers
were wonderful writers
(knew a dozen ways
to use a semicolon, and
could diagram the hell
out of a sentence)
they could really write
and write and write all day
but had
practically nothing to say

I switched majors right away—
(to Philosophy)

still wanted to write
but only things
worth reading,
and so I thought
TRUTH and LIGHT
always ring
int'resting—

creative or not.

Diamonds Mixed with Broken Glass

"These are precious jewels," I say,
with a hush in my voice, pouring
spark'ling nuggets into Ricky's
grubby hands. "Are these real," he asks,
still too young to constrain his awe.
"Yeah, numb-nuts, they're real," Logan says.

Ricky moves his palm, refracting
sunlight off and through each nugget.
The *gems* are for *Cops & Robbers*.
Ev'ry apartment complex kid
is designated good or bad,
police or a thief, wheat or chaff.

The apartments are redundant—
each unit just like the other;
the stove is here, the bathroom there,
but the folks inside are unique.
Oh, sure, they all feel the same heat,
but how they process it differs.

One time at Ricky's place his dad
gave us a huge cardboard box full
of snack-size potato chips and
cookies and snack crackers. He said:
"Help yourself. These expired today"

(he was a delivery guy
for a big time snack company).
He even grabbed a bag of chips
and sat with us as we pigged out
(it made me wish I had a dad).

Logan's dad was nothing like that.
I have no idea where *he* worked.
But one time we were playing games.
His dad came home mad as hell.
He was missing a beer, I guess,
and he grabbed Logan's wrist and pulled
him to the kitchen stovetop,
clicked on the electric burner,
and he held Logan's hand an inch
above the burning iron rings.

"Hold out your damn hand," his dad yelled.
"Do we take things that are not ours?"
Heat glowed red on Logan's small palm.
"I didn't take it," Logan wailed.
Then his dad looked right at *me*, yelled:
"Mind your own fucking business!"
I jerked my gaze away, cowered.
"Did you take my beer? Answer me!"
"Okay! Okay! I took your beer."

His dad yanked the hand off the heat
and shoved Logan back toward us.
"Goddamned kid," he said. Logan wept.
I realized, for the first time:
Not all fathers are real fathers,
and, if you can't have the real thing,
it's better to have none at all.

Anyway, we play Cops & Robbers.
The robbers have to steal the gems
from the top of the curly slide.
The cops have to tag the robbers
to put them in the pretend jail.
Logan always tries to cheat and
Ricky always gets distracted.
"What're they made of," Ricky asks,
still transfixed by all the jewels.

"It's a secret," I say. Logan
scoffs, "It's glass, that's all that they are."
Logan's right. That's all that they were.
Pieces of broken beer bottles
gathered from around the dumpster;
green and blue, clear and brown nuggets;
discarded chunks carefully washed;
broken shards made shiny to see;
worthless trash made beautiful.

haiku 8

"There's plenty of time."
That's what I want to hear, and:
"All those wounds will heal."

picking insects from my madness beard

(20 experiments in abstract verse)

The Representative

I represent the beggar
I brought all of my papers
The undersigned
Shall hereby drop said coin
In said cup
Take two steps back
Wink left eye
Giver shall attain receipt
For presentation to said Lord
The aforementioned beggar
Hereby expresses "thanks"
On said ledger
With borrowed pen
From unmentioned lender

All My Friends

Shuffling thoughts
Through cryptic boxes.
All that has been bound unwinds.
Connecting dots
Throuqh paradoxes.
All my friends have restless minds.

Switching assets
For greater angles.
Ev'ry path leads to extremes.
Shifting facets,
Avoiding tangles.
All my friends are chasing dreams.

Applying Psalms
with honest measures.
Ev'ry whole is made of parts.
Persistent calms
Through constant pressures.
All my friends have steady hearts.

Blistering feet
On taunted seekers.
Ev'ry traveler will plod.
Enduring heat
From holy speakers.
All my friends are seeking God.

the brain in the closet

I sit at my desk
my brain's in my closet
trying to construct a new
more creative thought

the door swings open
my brain exclaims:
"Sinners Love to Sled!"

I stomp my foot and yell
at my brain:

> *"Get back in there and don't come out*
> *unless you've something better than this,*
> *this, this, non-sense!"*

the door creaks open moments later
my brain emerges with a grin:
"Pencils Pulverize Pensive Oppressors."

I lurch to my feet and point:

> *"If I wanted silly alliteration*
> *I'd have gone to a grade school!*
> *Now, get back in there!"*

with a frown my brain closes
the closet door then re-emerges
with woe and contrition and says:

"Even if I could grasp a planet
spin it on my finger
you'll always want something more—
I could strap hair-brushes
to the hooves of dancing donkeys
to clean the teeth of Beluga Whales
and you'd stand wholly unimpressed."

my shoulders droop
my arms spread and
I embrace my brain
in a dramatic hug

"*oh, there-there...*" I say
and pull away:

> "*You know I love you, little guy.
> Hey! You're my little buddy, right?
> Where would I be without you?*"

my brain stands silent
shifts his gaze to the closet doors
where I am pointing as I say:

"*Now get back in there and try again.*"

metaphysical jazz

fire burns thru
parallel dimensions
that press against life.
what is a person
other than a short-
term temporary
contraction of matter
that waddles thru
the burning world
tryna' become some
thing that transcends?

it's all metaphysical
jazz and nobody knows
just how it will go.
we try not to think
about it but we can't
help it—we're poked
by a divide: a wide
wide wide variety
of possibility.

years? we might get
30 we might get 5.
we start epic projects
with no idea whether
we've got the time
to carry them across
the line.

Smart Phone

Drifting opinions explode
over crowded connector
circuits tickling our amygdala.
Pixels cast fantastic magic
images across glass canvases
rousing our occipital lobe.
Isolated stranger people
tapping understated feelings
into spiritless machines.
Finger pushers sliding pixel
objects all around the face
of our handheld digital door.

We lean and crouch
we peer way down
our eyes are locked upon
glowing wicked essences
like illuminated wombs
bending us over and in
crouching us and curling us
shrinking us and whittling us
down down down
until we find we are
now small enough
for our pocket-sized
aluminum tombs
our handheld glass caskets.

A Resurrection Year

It was a resurrection year
there were bags under my eyes
there were the burdens of my sins
there were those dangly pointy things
there were women on the verge
of drawing me in

it was a perplexity year
a year of scattered projects
and loose associations

self-righteous Bible-believers
quieted our Bible-scandals
and polished up our Bible-sandals
as over-wealthy hippy-chicks
took enlightened classes
then spewed curses at our tail-pipes
which were coughing filthy gasses

it was a year of shrinking walls—
I was peeking over the top
I was peering around the sides
I was dancing in the light
I was dancing in the light with
other immigrants—scattered
tenants returning to our homes
and not one of us danced alone

Beauty

Beauty is fleeting.
In fact, it's speeding.
Issue a ticket!
Beauty is neuter.
A bitch in the thicket.
A bastardly suitor.
Beauty is needy.
A grape in the thistles.
And the idiot whistles.
Beauty is precious
for the rich or the simple.
A heavenly message,
or an unholy symbol.
A dangerous passage
for the dumb or the nimble.

Things to Come

"I'm usually more cynical than this,"
said the man to the lady—
as a warning of things to come.
She thought it a compliment
and moved her hair with her thumb.
He was a bricklayer,
She was a stranger.
He moved her hair with his thumb.
"What… should I call you," asked he.
"Please do," said she.

(Her name was "What")

people are approachable

People are approachable,
but you have to do it right.
You can't just jump out at them
from behind the flag pole,
or spring up at them
from out of their hose-box.
You have to move smooth
and casual, like "it ain't nothing."
You can't bring up sad stories
or spew forth the drama of your past,
and they don't care about your drunk fathers
or your unsatisfiable mothers.
All they care about is their own wish lists
and their own to-do lists.
Approach them with a helping hand,
and they will invite you to dinner.
Approach them with a task
and they will darken the tone of their voice.
Approach them with intoxicated slur
and they will awkwardly back away.
Sober up then and wash yourself.
Prepare for your approach.
Come in smooth and offer a helping hand.

the social animal

people bog me down
they surround me
"Look at them all!"
they are sign-readers
vote-casters
they are anti-vagabonds
who scrape and wander
and go far below the speed limit—
"I can't get around them!"
I signal and blink
I cuss and shake
my head

I need people
I am a social animal
I'm designed for others
"These signs are made by people," I shout
I'm built to love
I'm incomplete
without a friend
"These stop signs are here to serve *us*!"

I am surrounded by sign-readers
and thieves who conceal their cheats
my car is a turbo-charged sedan
but there's never enough room
to really let that turbo blow
I am a social animal

Leave me alone

the syllabus

In this class you will overcome stupidity,
Conquer the monsters of your mind,
And shake hands with the future.
Learning will occur in non-competitive groups
Where you can impress strangers
With your uncanny wit,
And ponder insightful lectures
That will entertain you
And make you giggle.
You'll forget you are learning.

Grading is done on a curve.
Attendance is mandatory.

A Secret Gratitude

When all is said and done
(and when we cease our streams
of whiny bickering, and when
the well of our complaints run dry),
I feel I can be genuinely thankful,
if for nothing else,
that when the mighty earth,
in it's big, stupid orbit,
and with its rapid,
yet seemingly slow, doltish spin...
It is *here* that I can be thankful:

that the spinning earth
does not have
some kind
of high-pitched squeak.

How annoying would *that* be?
A mighty "Earth Squeak!"
How could anybody sleep?
We'd need research teams
to identify the sources,
then pour tons of oil (or butter)
into the suspect cavity or crevice.
And who knows how long
the noises would be halted?
The world only has so much oil.
And you know as well as I do:
governments would encourage
the breeding of cows for endless
supplies of butter—tax-breaks
and kick-backs for everybody
who breeds cows.

Pensive Vampire Cow

Independent Thinkers

Independent thinkers
see me on the street
and say: "Hello!"
But everyone says that.

Independent thinkers
greet me on the street
and shake my hand.
But everybody shakes my hand.

Independent thinkers
pass me on the street
and wave good-bye.
But everybody waves good-bye.

Independent thinkers
step across the tracks
and now they're gone,
and now I lost my train of thought.

the click

future folks when
clicking their things
that flicker and spin
will sit impressed
and consider us
lacking
depressed

> *Life must've been dull.*
> *Life must've been taxing.*
> *They must've been sicker.*
> *They must've been thin.*

—click—

...

—flicker—

...

...

—spin—

MAKE OTHERS SMILE

A smile is
an approval gesture.
We walk around
with our tender wounds
and our violin quartet
trying to ignite smiles on strangers—
especially beautiful ones,
healthy ones.
We do kind things despite our pain.
We ding the bell and scrape the shoe
(and nobody has to know anything).
We see the doctor and show her our poor health.
She tears the sheet and
scribbles out her perpetual prescription:

Make Others Smile

it says, and we fold it up
and put it in our pocket.

"Will my insurance cover it," we ask
(naive to all the new laws about healthcare and
money-payments).

"Yes. You're covered," she says,
and smiles

and
you begin feeling better already.

the fight

I'm creaky and ached
dragging limbs in the sunshine bake
it's not really a walk or a dance but a fight
—just to live another day
the way that I want
in the light
but stuff keeps piling up
useless crap I shouldn't have
project fragments tumble over
all my shelves and all my desks.

There's a temptation to twirl
in the center of the room
with a kerosine can in each hand
dousing all my bad ideas
dousing all my eggshell plans
just before dropping a match
on the waiting eruption
as I drag my limbs to the front yard
to watch it all
expand in anger
contract in shame
down to dry ash
to be fondled by every breeze
down to dimensions past
under doors without keys
all the way down to START AGAIN
down to nothing but an open space
—a fresh canvas face.

What could I do then?

this boat

I'm far less sure
about important things
than I used to be.

It's just that everyone's
so damned specialized and
supercilious.

I'm designing the newest
Noah's Ark just to sneak away
with my zoo society.

I'm varnishing wood planks
while brilliant pontificators are
wooing me with their brain tricks.

Bridges burn all around me
I hurry along the mast
with my hammer.

Nails are tapped
shutters attached.
"This boat will sail!"

Yet, I'm far less competent
than I used to be. I read.
I steal. I cheat.

My faith is a storm cloud
building up at sundown.
The woman is knitting.

The dog is chewing
an imitation bone. I pound
my hammer on the mast.

The clouds gather fast
and rumble as they darken
and it begins to rain

I lean out over the side
It is rising to consume me
I am dashing for the tool box.

"This boat will sail!"

I'm up to my ears in it
and far less secure
than I used to be.

hearts like houses

hearts like houses
a hundred years old
in forgotten prairies
without roads
tilting
creaking
faded gray
blown-out windows
vacant doorways
infested with ghosts
no one else knows.

a bizarre and scary dream

I was sipping Alabama Roasted Tea
with a good President of the United States.
I presented to him a flaming document
given to me by Alien counterintelligence,
and I warned him: "the moon is about to crumble
over Kentucky, and all the citizens and their
chickens will be crushed by moon chunks."

He said, *I know. I've already ordered*
General So-and-So
to promptly dispatch
the chemical clowns
to drunken all the townsfolk.

Then the President grabbed a spoonful of unicorn
mucus from a marble bowl
and spread it on his wheat toast.
Unicorn snot dripped from his lip to his chin
and a fly flew across the table and stuck to it.
I said, "Mr. President. Your chin, sir."
An agent named Daisy pinched off
the struggling fly and fed it to a toad
she kept in her coat pocket.

Our waitress came to refill our tea,
but she was yanked into the sky
by a shrieking Pterodactyl.
Her apron fluttered to the floor
and her high-heel shoe

splattered in my soup.
The President and I watched
the prehistoric creature
fly away with the kicking waitress,
and I said, "Ya' know, Mr. President,
good help is so hard to find."

A cellular phone jingled and the agent known as
'Can't' answered.
He whispered something
into the President's ear.
The President nodded.
"Thank you, agent Can't," he said.
The great President then looked at me,
"Peasant, is there a problem?"
I said, "Huh? Oh, I was just thinking
of a scary dream that woke me
screaming in the night."
What was it about, asked Daisy.
Tell us, ordered Can't.

"Well, I dreamt there were 7 days per week
and the citizens had to work 5 of them,
and there was only 24 hours in the day,
and we had to work 8 of those hours,
and it took an hour to get to work,
and another hour to get home,
because we all lived and worked
in the same places, at the same times
and on the same roads;
and we all told the same jokes

because entertainment was paid for
by 'advertisers,' who only supported programs
that *everyone* watched;
and the citizens waged war
on patches of weeds called grass,
and spent their evenings fighting
to make it green, and when it was greener
they'd yell "Not green enough!"
We all grew bored and uncomfortable,
and retaliated with rollercoasters
and nightclubs—that was all we had!
So we pretended
we were having more fun
than we really were.
And we pretended
careers were more important than they are.
And we thought happiness
was simply to be entertained,
and that life's great reward was retirement,
and that "getting old" meant
"not doing as much."

Daisy shivered and Can't convulsed.
The President shook his head:
*"What a bizarre and scary dream
you had last night, peasant."*

what I'm saying is, "Goodnight."

Pass me thru a portal of pillows,
where impromptu playwrights
confront me with surrealistic pictures,
and I hustle to solve the false
histories and quack narratives of
melatonin's provocative dimensions.

Yes, hurry me to slumber's chamber,
where soft jackhammers & hushed
vacuums cleanse death-crust
from my eyes, where blessed cherubs
soothe and bandage
all of my brainstorm wounds.

Where cognitive accountants
reverse the day's curses, where
neuronal janitors sweep debris,
and sponge up surplus fragments
of a frantic day, and process all
the traumas of my panic lifestyle.

Might I descend deep into ancient
caverns of sleep, spaces so deep
they awaken the Id, and unleash
kinetic Rorschach tests that
confront my psyche, while
burning matches rain down,
to illuminate my soul enigmas.

My heart howls with flames as they
lower me slowly into kerosene
dreams—where my psyche's prodded,
my reactions measured, and strange
episodes test my mettle, and I stand
before the actual size of my crises.

Might I stand firm in that arena, where
the concierges of my subconscious
service me with virtual reality, to
unmask & conquer my false ego
as I step strong, yet light, thru each
ambiguously terrifying doorway.

Until wide rainbows burst forth
from laughing neurotransmitters,
upon which I slide down, down,
down to sunrise; back to my bed,
back to the false culture, where
the distracted masses prod me
with their dazzle sticks, enchant
me with their miracle objects, and
try to contort and corrupt me—
having absolutely no idea all
that I had endured, discovered,
and overcome the night before.

seminary poems
2001–2007

(my search for God
at Bethel Seminary)

"Go to Bethel and sin..."

Amos 4:4

Docks and Mailboxes

It's a change that I can make.
The Lord's promises do not fail.
I long to sit on the dock at the lake.
I long for letters in my mail.

Hezekiah did not want to die.
The Lord hears a righteous plea.
A tombstone and a buzzing fly.
"I'm not yet who I want to be."

The city streets are always bright.
The Lord gave Judas wine and bread.
Even bugs are drawn to light,
Where well placed spiders get well fed.

Adam and Eve could've done better.
The Lord's chances are not fake.
How long 'til someone writes a letter?
How long did Adam's grieving take?

I like it when the lake is calm.
The Lord will finish what He starts.
Which was David's favorite Psalm?
The Lord will heal our wounded hearts.

Time is not a 'thing'

If you hit the door face first
while fumbling for the switch
you might shout "Ouch!"
your back will slouch
your head will ring
a door can be an awful thing.

Or if you pick your nose in school
and it's clinging to your pinky
you might think "Dang"
and shake your hand
"Why won't this bugor fling?"
A bugor is a sticky thing.

But no one's ever hit
their face upon an "hour"
or stumbled on a "week"
a 'day' won't bite
a 'month' won't sting—

Time
is not a 'thing'!

You may find clocks or calendars
while at the mall to buy a gift
but those are just for measurement
like a ruler or thermometer
measures 'degree' or 'inch'

You'll not find 40-seconds

stuck upon your thumb
or see a *weekend* blowing
through your yard—
the thought of it is dumb.

Time is neither linear nor circular
nor quasi-pseudo-pentatuchialar
one can't be in it or above it
as a finger in a ring
or a puppetmaster dangling string—

Time is not a thing!

Come one
come all
Arminians,
Come and help me sing:

"Baw-Daw-Boopty-Woopty-Bing—
Time is NOT a Thing!"

Hannah is not drunk
(I Samuel 1:13)

Hannah prays in her heart,
that's why you can't see her lips moving.
Hannah keeps herself apart.
She guards her heart
from darkness shards.
Hannah finds a way.
She shuffles through the crowds.
She goes through places she is not allowed.
Hannah shuffles through the storm
with no coat to keep her warm,
with no umbrella to keep her dry.
She's constructing a song.
She's formulating a prayer.
She prays her prayers deep inside.
Hannah shuffles up to higher grounds.
Jacob saw a stairway to heaven
and there was Hannah coming down.
She did not see him wave
as she shuffled through the crowds,
set apart in private thoughts,
shuffling through the town.
She does her work and rarely frowns.
Her lips only move when she chews,
or when she's bringing happy news,
or when confronting dark proposals
from all the city's clowns.
She prays her prayers in her heart
and prays a prayer for the crowds
as she goes through places she is not allowed.

The Angry Evangelist

Now do you believe, you fool?
You've got the word slapped against your cheek!
Rub that sting!
What do you seek?
The mountains sing!

Now do you believe, you thief?
You've got our hope on a pinwheel in your brain.
Spin that wheel!
Are you so vain?
The hope is real!

Don't you yet believe, you dolt?
You've got to open a window to feel a breeze.
Let it blow!
It's yours to seize!
It's yours to know!

Believe! Believe! You sinking stone!
You've got the dagger of proof poking your eye!
Lose the sheath!
Do angels lie?
Believe! Believe!

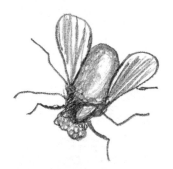

Ghosts of Flies

"Do we carry disease around,
Or, are *we* the disease ourselves?"
    For that there's much debate
    Within the world of flies.

Some say there are unseen forces
To which they crash (some think it glass).
    Things they can't contemplate
    Despite their many eyes.

Either way, they fear the spider,
Who'll leave them hollow, haunted shells.
    "We see his web too late;
    It beckons our demise."

Though many find it fickle hope,
Some say the spider's days are few—
    Though no one knows the date
    Or how the spider dies.

Prophets say the beast will tangle
Within the web he made himself—
    As written on a slate
    And given to the wise.

And flies will rise from ages past,
The Beast of Webs will become trapped.
    In fear will face his fate:
    Consumed by ghosts of flies.

The Drifter

A dimwit sold me potion
And I drunk it.
I rowed my boat onto the ocean
And I sunk it!
Now I'm passed-out naked on the shore.
"I don't want to be a sailor anymore."

I took a job and had a boss—
Just for money!
He yelled until his eyes would cross—
It was funny!
But now my back aches as I scrub his floor.
"I don't want to be a worker anymore."

So I went before a woman and wept—
She was pleasing.
She said she loved me as we slept—
She was teasing!
Now my money's gone, my heart is sore.
"I don't want to be a lover anymore."

I got lost among the masses in the streets
Of Galilee
And I am one whom Jesus meets
Under a tree.
I asked him: "Where's the nearest store?"
He said he knows of all my worthless days

And all my grief,
And all my futile vagrant ways—
"And life is brief."
I asked him if we'd met somewhere before.
He said: "Drifter, I'm your God and Lord."

He said: "You have a soul,
and I will seal it."
I said: "It's just an empty hole."
He said: "I'll heal it."
But I've been duped by promises before,
And I don't want to be The Sucker anymore.

He promised me abundant life.
But like a thief,
They killed him on a cross of strife,
And life is brief.
Then I'm lost again out in the streets
Of Galilee
And I am one whom Jesus meets
Under a tree.
I shake my head and wipe my eyes—
All he said he meant!
I confessed: "My life is ripe with lies."
He said: "Repent."
Now I kneel before him on the floor.
"I don't want to be a drifter anymore."

Electric Bird Unplugged

haiku 9

an elephant poops
Noah checks the food supply
it begins to rain

Seeking God in America
(a poetic prayer circa 2002)

My Lord, your words, they knock me down.
They parse and pester all my thoughts.
They make my every move profound.
I know without these words I'm lost.
And though I know that I've been found,
At times I wonder: *at what cost?*

Because hours are made of minutes,
And minutes are made of seconds,
Which can be split without limit
And still never find the present—
Yet we still exist within it
(in moments beyond assessment).

And *now* always slips into *then*.
Within each *now* that passes by
Are many things that could have been
And many things I could have tried.
But *now* always returns again,
Without delay, without divide.

Within each *now* are great debates,
Where electrified chemical
Forms feelings and urges and aches—
That lobby and surge, push and pull,
And coalesce to conscious states
In secret courtrooms of my skull.

What consciousness is, who can tell?
Existence's window or door?
A show to see and feel and smell?
Power to be and to explore?
Far too complex for *one* brain cell.
Yet, too intact for any more.

And in the midst of all of this
(Upon the icy slope of time—
From moments we cannot assess—
From in the miracle of mind—
Which no one knows just where it is),
We're called to live a certain life.

A life that we can freely choose.
Some choices I've made have raised me,
And gave me wisdom I can use.
Some choices I've made were crazy,
And most of what I'd gain I'd lose—
Both angels and demons praise me!

And like the others, I am lost,
Yet keep going where I'm going—
Harassed and helpless to my wants,
Like tissue in the wind, blowing;
Seeking only the lowest cost
To slow debts that won't stop growing.

There's too much opportunity,
Creating aches from brain to bone,
That scatters all community
As each one works to get their own—
Despite the known futility
Of trading sweat for wine and gold.

We have our goods made overseas,
And pay with pennies, threats, and scars.
Our stickers say: "Imagine Peace."
Pasted upon imported cars—
So each of us becomes a thief,
That masturbates our stupid hearts.

But factories keep filling stores
With band-aids, guns, tombstones and drugs.
The stockholders all hope for wars—
Like lawyers might hope for thugs,
Like preachers shaking fists at whores,
Like crop-dusters might hope for bugs.

A *system* of self-centeredness
(earth's limitation is the fuel—
Ignited by our certain deaths,
That makes us selfish, scared, and cruel).
Where poverty and anger spreads,
And envy mocks the Golden Rule.

It's all a game of want and theft
Where everyone becomes a guard.
I sob and think myself bereft
Because the hand I'm dealt is hard.
Nothing like your servant Joseph
Who praised your name with ev'ry card.

From heaven's gate to Satan's perch
You can hear the sounds of laughter,
That we would trade eternal worth
To appease our earthly captor
(There are no Josephs in the church —
Just religious slaves and masters).

And the religious love to lose,
How they love to be "convicted,"
And lick the soles of sinner's shoes,
Then preach cures for being wicked,
And practice love in Sunday Schools —
Where those they hate are forbidden.

The congregation thinks they're bad —
So bad that they can not choose good.
They form *Theologies of Can't*
(While even Moses says they could).
So each becomes a sycophant —
Just like the serpent said they would.

They claim that you're "too big to know,"
Then raise their hands up high and shout:
"The Spirit's moving in my soul!"
And claim: "The Lord has helped me out!"
As if they basked in Eden's glow,
As if you never kicked us out!

But Lord, your words, they call me out.
They straighten all my crooked thoughts.
They challenge every foolish doubt.
They show me all that I have sought.
They show me what life's all about
(The life humanity forgot).

Life too pure for non-believers
(Whose hassled hearts can only feign—
Their spirits grow ever weaker,
A spit into a hurricane).
It's a life just for the Seekers,
Who'll usher in your Holy reign,

Who'll live under your holy trance,
With eyes that make your will distinct,
To rise above our circumstance,
Whereat our souls and yours are linked,
To nullify the devil's chance,
And watch his kingdoms slowly sink.

And see the cosmic forces shift:
When righteousness and justice meet,
When death and limitation lift,
And chaff is burned away from wheat,
And ev'ry curse becomes a gift
That's set before our Savior's feet.

But, Lord, my soul is still a mess.
I see your hand, but can't grab it.
I'm tangled in the devil's nets,
Flailing like a wounded rabbit
(Distracted by a stupid stress—
Swindled by my ancient habits).

I thought I was a rolling stone,
And thought that I was roaming free.
I went about my life alone.
But I was just a tumbleweed.
So now I'm coming to your throne,
I'm seeking your community.

Which is spread through many churches,
Like diamonds mixed with broken glass,
Found by anyone who searches
(Who can separate weed from grass),
Until the *real* church emerges,
And all the insincere shall pass.

I was among the billiard balls,
But now I am the butterfly
That flutters over waterfalls.
I've found my eye behind my eyes
And windows where there once were walls
It's given me the will to try.

To try to tolerate disdain.
The will to free myself from debt.
To try to live without complaint,
And be content with what I get.
To reap the harvest of a saint
(The only harvest worth its sweat).

I'll learn to dwell on doing right,
And make my ev'ry action count.
Each word I speak will give off light—
Extracted from your Holy fount.
Teach me, Lord, both day and night:
To live the Sermon on the Mount.

To rise up from my gravity,
Until I'm out of Satan's range.
To fill up ev'ry cavity
Created by a life estranged.
To overcome depravity,
As one whose heart has really changed.

You've snatched me from the living grave.
This chance I have won't be wasted.
I let myself become a slave
(It's my own fault—I will face it).
You've promised freedom for the saved.
It's so close I almost taste it!

It's here in the air between us.
The devil stumbles, demons slip—
Hear their urgent whispers seek us.
Hear the Pharisees crack their whips
(Even when the Lord has freed us
And destiny has lost its grip).

Your Spirit burns and will not tire,
Consuming all un-holy threat,
And drawing out divine desire
In those whose hearts your Spirit lit—
I've got that fire!
I'm not dead yet!

You can follow Dan at:

twitter.com/thatdankent

Other books by Dan Kent:

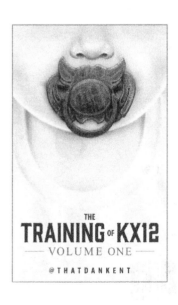

Made in the USA
Monee, IL
15 April 2025

15821772R00115